The Anastasia File

A Play

Royce Ryton

Samuel French – London
New York – Sydney – Toronto – Hollywood

4. Rights of Performance by Amateurs are controlled by SAMUEL FRENCH LTD, 52 FITZROY STREET, LONDON W1P 6JR, and they, or their authorized agents, issue licences to amateurs to give performances of this play on payment of a fee. **It is an infringement of the Copyright to give any performance or public reading of the play before the fee has been paid and the licence issued.**

5. Licences are issued subject to the understanding that it shall be made clear in all advertising matter that the audience will witness an amateur performance; that the names of the authors of the plays shall be included on all announcements and on all programmes; and that the integrity of the author's work will be preserved.

The Royalty Fee indicated below is subject to contract and subject to variation at the sole discretion of Samuel French Ltd.

Basic fee for each and every performance by amateurs in the British Isles — Code M

In Theatres or Halls seating Six Hundred or more the fee will be subject to negotiation.

In Territories Overseas the fee quoted above may not apply. A fee will be quoted on application to our local authorized agent, or if there is no such agent, on application to Samuel French Ltd, London.

6. The Professional Rights in this play are controlled by MICHAEL IMISON (PLAYWRIGHTS) LTD, 28 Almeida Street, London N1.

The publication of this play does not imply that it is necessarily available for performance by amateurs or professionals, either in the British Isles or Overseas. Amateurs and professionals considering a production are strongly advised in their own interests to apply to the appropriate agents for consent before starting rehearsals or booking a theatre or hall.

ISBN 0 573 01642 9

THE ANASTASIA FILE

First performed under the title *I Am Who I Am* at the Arts Theatre, Cambridge, on 15th August, 1978, with the following cast of characters:

Inspector	Laurence Payne
Men	Roger Hume
Mrs Manahan	Beth Ellis
Women	Judy Wilson

The play directed by Joan Kemp-Welch
Designed by Tanya McCallin

Subsequently performed under the title *The Anastasia File* at the Derby Playhouse, in association with North Bank Productions, on 5th February, 1986, with the following cast of characters:

Mrs Manahan	Angela Down
Inspector	William Marlowe
Actor	Colin Bennett
Actress	Judy Wilson

The play directed by Chris Hayes
Designed by Belinda Ackermann

PRODUCTION NOTES

SETTINGS

The stage is set as simply as possible, a couple of chairs, a table, a coat stand. That is all that is needed, for the stage represents a variety of places—a hospital, an office, various private drawing-rooms.

CASTING

The Inspector and Mrs Manahan are themselves throughout the play, but the Actor and Actress play a variety of parts, nurses, friends, secretaries, doctors, patients. The coat stand is used for them to hang a variety of coats, hats and other props which they use and put on when they change characters. It is also important that when they change characters, there is always a slight difference in their appearance and clothes and in their voices.

ACT I*

The Inspector's office

The Inspector is seated at his desk working. He is a man of about forty. He is very pleasant and efficient and kind

The Actor comes in as a police officer

Actor Mrs Manahan is here, sir.
Inspector Oh yes. Show her in.

The Actor exits

The Inspector rises. He seems a little nervous. He places a chair C *stage and waits*

Mrs Manahan comes in. No longer young, she has a certain indefinable presence

Mrs Manahan.

She stands and looks at him silently

Would you care to sit down?

She sits

Well, you see ...
Mrs Manahan I would know you anywhere, young man. You are very like your father.
Inspector So my mother always told me. He had a moustache, of course.
Mrs Manahan He is dead?
Inspector Oh yes. Before the war. My mother died recently too and I have been going through all her papers—which of course included his things as well and I discovered his notes on you.
Mrs Manahan And you want to ask me a whole lot of questions? And I have never met anyone who did not want to ask me questions. They write books and newspaper articles. They defend me. They attack me. It seems to me that the world is consumed with curiosity about me and will remain so for the rest of time. And I will tell you why. They do not want the answer. They want the mystery. They want to say to each other "I wonder what the truth is" far more than they want the truth. Romantics believe me, cynics still doubt me, but I have ceased to care. I came to see you for two reasons.
Inspector And what are they?
Mrs Manahan Because your father was very kind to me all those years ago,

*N.B. Paragraph 3 on page ii of this Acting Edition regarding photocopying and video-recording should be carefully read.

and to ask you to leave me alone. I am old, Inspector, and tired, Inspector—besides I have said all there is to say years ago. I am married again and have a legal name no one can challenge. I have even found a little happiness in a new life. Please Inspector, leave me alone.

Inspector My father said you always told the truth—he searched for the truth and so do I, that's why we both became policemen. Yours is an unsolved case. He wanted to solve it. It became an obsession with him. I have inherited that obsession, and I tell you something, you wanted it solved too, otherwise you wouldn't be here. That's why you always see people in the end. Somewhere deep inside you there's a hope that the key to the mystery will be unearthed.

Mrs Manahan (*rising*) No, you are quite wrong. Because you see, to me there is no mystery. I know the answer.

Inspector There have been many books about you, I'm thinking of writing a book, no—not about you, it'll be quite different—in nineteen-fourteen Germany invaded Belgium—and France and England were swept by stories of German atrocities in Belgium. After the war a court of inquiry was held, not one atrocity could be authenticated. Not one. I've often thought of publishing a book called, "The atrocities that never were".

Mrs Manahan comes back, puts her coat on the coat stand and sits again

Mrs Manahan And you think my life is a mystery that never was ... very well then, what is it you want to know?

Black-out

The Lights go up again at once

The Inspector and Mrs Manahan are not there, but the Actor and Actress are. The Actor is seated. The Actress standing. They wear white coats

Actor as Doctor A Nurse, hand me that police file, will you?
Actress as Nurse A Which one, Doctor?
Actor The attempted suicide.
Actress We have four ... The Baron von ...
Actor No no. The girl.
Actress The one found in the canal?
Actor That's it. What's her name?
Actress We don't know.
Actor Hasn't she spoken?
Actress Not once. Vague indistinct murmurings, that's all.
Actor No papers on her?
Actress I don't think so.
Actor (*glancing at the file*) When was she found?
Actress The twenty-seventh of February.
Actor A week ago. Ah! What do the police say? (*He reads the report*) Unknown girl's attempted suicide. Yesterday evening on the twenty-seventh of February nineteen-twenty at nine p.m. a girl of about twenty jumped off the Bendler Bridge into the Canal with the intention of taking her life. She was saved by a police sergeant and admitted to the Elisabeth

Hospital . . . etc. etc . . . no papers on her . . . and so forth—she refused to make any statements. Well, I'd better go and look at her.

The Actress exits and wheels in Mrs Manahan in a hospital bed. She is staring vacantly ahead of her, presumably comprehending nothing

Actress She doesn't speak at all, Doctor.
Actor Where's her temperature chart, Nurse?
Actress Here, Doctor.
Actor One doesn't know how much she understands. What is your name? We don't want to hurt you, what is your name?
Actress She understands German. I'm sure of it. When we tell her to wash or get out of bed for us to make it, she does so.
Actor Does she talk in her sleep?
Actress She calls out. I can't make out the words.
Actor Do you have any relatives? Do you know anyone in Berlin? What is she doing?
Actress She always hides like that if one talks to her for long.
Actor I suppose she's not pretending.
Actress I certainly don't think so.
Actor And yet . . . I don't know—of course I'm not a specialist in mental cases, but I don't think she's mad. She'd better go to the Dalldorf Asylum. Arrange the transfer, will you?

The Actor crosses to the desk and sits. He presses a bell then calls out "Next Please"

The Actress helps Mrs Manahan out of bed and crosses with her to the desk

Where is she from?
Actress as Nurse B The Elisabeth Hospital, sir.
Actor as Doctor B What's her name?
Actress They don't know.
Actor Don't know?
Actress She was found in a canal by the police. Apparently she had no identification papers and she won't speak.
Actor They've made inquiries and advertised, I suppose?
Actress Oh yes. No one has come forward.
Actor We live in very strange times. (*He gets up and crosses to Mrs Manahan*) I suppose she did jump. She wasn't pushed.
Actress I think it's most unlikely. She'd have said if she was pushed.
Actor (*slowly and carefully*) How old are you?

Silence

What is your name?

Silence

Actress Why don't you speak, dear? We won't hurt you or be in any way unkind. We want to help you.

The Actor starts a medical examination. He looks into her eyes, into her mouth, at her ears. He lifts her arms and lets them drop

Actor It's difficult to estimate her age, she's dreadfully thin. (*He moves to take her wrist*)

Mrs Manahan shrinks in terror

Actress The Elisabeth Hospital said she often did that. It's as if she's trying to ward off blows.
Actor I won't hurt you.

Mrs Manahan sits. The Actor looks at her head, folding back the hair

Actor She's been in some form of street fighting. She's been hit in the head.
Actress She's been stabbed too, some time ago. There are stab wounds on the right side. She holds out the right arm with ease, the left with difficulty.
Actor Stand her up.

Mrs Manahan stands

So you understand me? Hold out your arms. Can't you straighten it?

Mrs Manahan calls out with pain

You'd better put her to bed.

The Actress leads her back to the bed. The Actor looks puzzled and watches her all the time. The Actress returns

Actor The arm may be tubercular. Arrange for tests to be taken.
Actress Yes doctor.
Actor Well, I don't know. I don't believe the patient is mad as such. Rather is she suffering from alienation of a depressive character. She's unquestionably been the victim of some sort of violence.
Actress That's possible.

They cross to her again

Actor How has she been?
Actress Improving steadily, I think.
Actor Walking at all?
Actress Oh yes. Sometimes she sits out on the balcony. She washes herself now and yesterday she had her first proper bath.
Actor Oh, splendid.
Actress Takes quite an interest in life too—judging from her smiles. But of course she's not speaking yet.
Actor Not at all?
Actress No.
Actor Is she eating more?
Actress Oh yes. Put on a little weight too.
Actor That's good, at any rate.
Actress I don't know how to put it—but she's co-operative. If she's silent, it's not a sullen silence. It's quite polite. Oh dear, I feel if we could only reach her, we'd like her.
Actor I'd like to see her walk.

Actress The doctor would like to see you walk about a bit, dear.

Mrs Manahan gets up quite readily and walks about

Actor She understands perfectly.
Actress Do you notice something, Doctor? She walks well. Look at that turn. She's very graceful.
Actor Well?
Actress I think she's been taught deportment.

They are now either side of her

Actor I agree. Despite her thinness and her whole appearance, she's been well cared for. Sit down again, will you please? I want to look at your feet. (*He examines the feet*) Yes, I'm right. They've had treatment. Expert treatment too. There's no doubt about it, she comes from a rich family.

They move away from her. She watches anxiously

That's what's so extraordinary about her. I mean, if she comes from a rich family why aren't they looking for her? She's been here a year now and not one enquiry from anyone, not one answer to an advertisement.
Actress Perhaps she isn't German.
Actor That's an idea.
Actress The Matron wondered if she was a refugee. She's not only been well brought up, she's been strictly brought up. She's very modest. She washes most carefully. She's very clean in her habits. I'd think she'd been taught in a convent if she didn't cross herself the wrong way.
Actor How do you mean?
Actress Right to left instead of left to right. Like so.
Actor Then she's Orthodox. They do that. (*He crosses to her*) Would you like to get back into bed?
Mrs Manahan Yes.

Silence

Actor (*very gently*) So you can speak.
Mrs Manahan Yes.
Actor And German too?
Mrs Manahan A little.
Actor But you're not German.

She is silent

Where do you come from? What happened to you in your native country?

She is silent

Have you any relatives? What did you run away from?

Mrs Manahan covers her face in her hands and tries to hide

Actress It's no use, Doctor. Once she does that, it's hopeless.
Actor Put her back to bed.
Actress Come along now. There's a good girl.

The Actress puts Mrs Manahan to bed and exits

The Actor crosses to the desk and sits

The Inspector comes in. He is, in fact, the 1st Inspector's father. He has a moustache and is wearing clothes which would be very correct for 1922

Actor Ah, Inspector.
Inspector It's good of you to see me again.
Actor Not at all. I'm most interested in this case. Have you made any progress?
Inspector I've drawn a complete blank everywhere. I've tried every possible hotel and almost every boarding house. No single girl registered anywhere. Any possible family visiting Berlin with a daughter between sixteen and twenty-five has been checked. No daughter is missing. Berlin families have all been checked too.
Actor She's not German.
Inspector How do you know?
Actor She's beginning to talk. Just a little.
Inspector Good. Now I can question her.
Actor No, no, you can't. She gets frightened and does this extraordinary hiding action, crouching and covering her face. She's been ill-treated, hit, stabbed and knocked about. You can't question her yet.
Inspector Has she been raped?
Actor No, but she's not a virgin.
Inspector She couldn't be quite simply a tart?
Actor No, no, no. She's far too modest.
Inspector I've known some very demure tarts in my time.
Actor Everything about her is virtuous, not to say prudish. If she's a tart the world is square, you're a woman and I'm the Kaiser. No, no. On the other hand she's had a baby.
Inspector You're sure.
Actor Quite. There are physical changes in a woman when she's had a baby and she's got them all. One or two could be coincidence but not all of them.
Inspector So we have a young woman, frightened, suicidal, mother of a child, from a rich family, victim of violence, alone in Berlin, February nineteen-twenty and no one reports her missing, no one cares, no one asks for her and she won't tell us anything. When she talks, what does she say?
Actor Yes please. No thank you. I am feeling better. I am not so well. Nothing, nothing about herself other than that.
Inspector The accent?
Actor Indefinable. It's quite good German, but it's taught. On the other hand she's often heard it spoken. She understands everything.
Inspector (*moving away to exit*) Let me know any fresh developments, Doctor.
Actor There is one thing.
Inspector Yes?
Actor She's very religious and prays.

Inspector So?
Actor She crosses herself in the Orthodox fashion.
Inspector Greek Orthodox?
Actor Yes.
Inspector She's not Greek. At least she doesn't look it. Still, it narrows the field a bit. She's not Jewish, Roman Catholic or Protestant. It narrows the nationality down too. There may be Orthodox Portuguese or Danes, but it's unlikely. Romanian? No. Polish?
Actor Catholic.
Inspector Serb?
Actor I've thought of Russian, but she doesn't look it.
Inspector She looks German to me. Try her out with various foreign languages. It might give us a lead. I don't mind admitting this case is beginning to intrigue me.

He exits

Mrs Manahan is seated reading

The Actress comes in

Actress Time to take your temperature. I'll pop it into your mouth. There ... what's that you're reading? An English magazine ... interesting?

Mrs Manahan nods happily

What are we today? Let's look. Quite normal. Those pills have helped a lot, haven't they, dear ...
Mrs Manahan I'm much better. There's nowhere near as much pain in my arm.
Actress Good. I wish I could speak English. I'm trying to learn it. (*Very slowly*) 'Ow do you do, Mrs Brown? It is very hot today. Can I have some tea, please?

Mrs Manahan laughs

What are you laughing at?
Mrs Manahan Your English. You have such a funny accent.

The Actress smiles vaguely and walks away. Then she crosses briskly to the Actor at his desk

Actress It worked. I left the magazines about as you suggested. French, Spanish, Italian, English. She took an English one and I found her reading it.
Actor Understanding it too?
Actress Obviously. Well, then I said I was learning English—and I am—so I spoke a few phrases and she laughed and I asked her why, and she said my accent was funny. I think she speaks English very well indeed.
Actor English? She can't be English. What would an English girl of good family be doing in Berlin in nineteen-twenty? The war was only just over. Businessman's child? Diplomat's daughter? They'd go to the police.
Actress Perhaps she married a German?

Actor When? Before nineteen-fourteen she'd be too young—and I'm certain she's had a child. She can't have married a German before nineteen-nineteen because of the war—so she'd a year to marry, have a child and get stranded and lost, be beaten up, stabbed, knocked about and commit suicide. It's out of the question. No, no. Continue with the Inspector's instructions. Chatter to her easily and happily, but don't ask questions, they make her suspicious.

The Actor exits

Actress Of course not doctor. (*She walks briskly to Mrs Manahan*) And how are we this morning?
Mrs Manahan Much better.
Actress Nurse tells me you've eaten quite a big breakfast. How splendid.
Mrs Manahan I love the autumn, don't you? It's looking so lovely out. I do hope I will soon be allowed to go for walks.
Actress The doctor's so pleased with you, it won't be long now. I shall be having to decide about my holiday soon.
Mrs Manahan Surely you have your holiday in the summer?
Actress Usually. I love winter sports so much though. I'm taking mine in the winter this year. My friend wants me to go to Sweden or Norway where, of course, the skiing is lovely and I want to go to Switzerland. Of course, it will be more expensive.
Mrs Manahan Why?
Actress Further away, but we can get a cheap pension. Then there's the rate of exchange. That's a worry too.
Mrs Manahan Oh, is travelling expensive?
Actress Enormously.
Mrs Manahan Gracious. I never knew that. I used to travel quite a lot once.
Actress I love trains.
Mrs Manahan It's funny, as a little girl, though I was often train sick, I was never sea sick.

The Actress is silent, she dare not ask a question

Of course, Papa's yacht was an excellent sea boat so we were lucky. I'd love to go to Switzerland with you. It must be lovely.

The Actress can't resist a question

Actress You've never been there?
Mrs Manahan No, no.
Actress Of course, I'm nervous about going abroad at all.
Mrs Manahan Why?
Actress Germans are not popular abroad. They tell such lies about us. The French I mean. They say we started the war. Such nonsense. Germany was encircled.
Mrs Manahan That's not true. Your Kaiser was so aggressive making all those threats. Then he should never have allied himself to Austria like that. Austria would never have delivered such an outrageous ultimatum to the King of Serbia without your Kaiser's backing. Russia had to keep her word and defend Serbia. She had a treaty with her she had to honour.

The Actress is staring at her amazed. Mrs Manahan suddenly realizes what she's said and stares back appalled. She also understands she's fallen into a trap

Actress Who are you?

Mrs Manahan retreats, she cringes into her chair, covers her face in her hands and tries to hide. She relapses in terror like earlier attitudes when first in hospital

The Actress leaves her side still staring at her

Mrs Manahan I nearly gave myself away. Papa, Papa, I mentioned Papa. But that was earlier. That was earlier, earlier. The Kaiser, what did I say about the Kaiser? I must keep calm, keep calm, keep calm. (*She picks up a paper and starts to try and read it. Her hands are trembling violently. She turns over a few pages blindly. Suddenly she stops and reads intently. Far from calming her, this sends her into raging hysterics. She flings the paper down*) The Bolsheviks demand return of all Russian citizens—no. No. No. I can't, I can't. Don't make me. God help me.

Actress (*rushing to her*) Calm down. Calm down. That's a good girl. What is it? What is it? Tell me what the matter is, tell me, oh please tell me.

Mrs Manahan subsides onto the floor moaning, her hands move frenziedly as if warding off blows and then she becomes silent. The Actress helps her onto her chair where she sits staring apathetically into space

Actress Just shut your eyes and rest and I'll be back in a little while.

She exits

The Actor appears with the Inspector

The Actress joins them

Actress It was most extraordinary. She was talking lucidly, clearly, authoritatively even.

Inspector Authoritatively?

Actress Yes. I have never seen anything like it. I really am quite shattered.

The Actress moves with the Inspector to near the desk

The Actor works on Mrs Manahan and gives her an injection

Actress I was chattering to her as you said, she'd been eating well, she wanted to be allowed out.

Inspector She was quite happy?

Actress Perfectly. Absolutely normal. I talked about going abroad.

Inspector Well?

Actress She doesn't understand the cost of things and I can tell you why. She has been very, very rich indeed.

Inspector How do you know?

Actress Papa had a yacht.

Inspector A yacht? Well that, of course, could be anything from a small sailing boat to a luxury steam yacht.

Actress It was a good sea boat.
Inspector Probably large then.

The Actor joins them

Actor I'm afraid we're right back to the beginning again. She's shut everything off.
Actress I'm so sorry doctor.
Inspector Papa had a yacht. A big one we think. A good sea boat.
Actor I'm sure it's not your fault, Sister. She's bound to have these setbacks from time to time. What actually caused the breakdown?
Actress I talked about going abroad. I mentioned the war, then I said Germans were unpopular abroad and that we'd been encircled by enemies and she flatly contradicted me. She knew the whole political background—she knew about Serbia and the Austrian ultimatum and she was quite distinctly anti-German. I said, "Who are you?" She stared in terror, she tried to calm herself, then she picked up a paper, read something and went quite, quite mad.
Inspector Something in the paper? Can you get it?
Actress Yes. (*She crosses to Mrs Manahan*)
Inspector If you have yachts, you are enormously rich. If you are that rich your family makes fusses if you vanish.
Actor Perhaps they're not that rich any more.
Actress Here we are.
Inspector What page?
Actress I don't know. Front page I suppose.
Inspector Might be anything ... Queen of Romania visits sister ... New National Socialist Party ... Bolshevik Government demands return of Russians. ... What's this? American millionaire in search ... Oh looking for ancestors ... This is no good, it might be anything. Well we've got one step forward—if Papa had a big enough yacht before the war it will be registered. I can check on that. If they're rich enough they'll be in Social Registers.

He exits, followed by the Actress

Actor (*crossing to Mrs Manahan*) You've recovered quicker from our little set-back than I thought.
Mrs Manahan Yes.
Actor Eating well?
Mrs Manahan Yes.
Actor How is the arm?
Mrs Manahan Better.
Actor Not very talkative, are we?
Mrs Manahan No.
Actor Oh well. (*He decides to go on trying*) You know we're only trying to help you. You clearly remember something about the past.

She is silent

You must have had relations and friends once.

She is silent

Someone must have cared for you at one time.

She starts to cry

Did you have any brothers and sisters?

She retreats and hides

Unless you tell us something we can't help you.

The Inspector enters and paces about

The Actress comes in. She no longer has her white coat on and looks as different as she can from the nurse she's been playing hitherto. Her hair perhaps is swept back

Inspector You know of our problem, Fraulein Hoede? Of our mystery?
Actress as Fraulein Hoede The whole hospital talks of nothing else.
Inspector I'm sure. Have you met her?
Actress Indeed. I take books and magazines to her as I take to all other patients. I try to interest her in games and in the outside world.
Inspector What do you make of her?
Actress She is unquestionably a real lady. She is always perfectly amiable but sometimes if displeased she can be haughty.
Inspector What interests her?
Actress Politics do. She is knowledgeable. She seldom if ever talks of them, but she reads political articles with interest. I can tell.
Inspector You speak several languages?
Actress Oh yes.
Inspector Well?
Actress Very well. My father was in the German consular service and served in France and England and for a very long time in Russia—in Yalta—and of course before the war in Argentina. He always insisted we went to local schools and I have a natural ear for languages.
Inspector Is she German?
Actress No, no. Her German is excellent, but not her native language.
Inspector English or French?
Actress I would hardly think so. She could be Russian. There was a very wealthy and quite large business class particularly around Moscow of course. Her father could be a business man with some political interests or appointments.
Inspector She mentioned a yacht.
Actress Many well-to-do Russians had a summer place in the Baltic.
Inspector Try her suddenly with Russian. Don't question her. Slip from German to Russian without warning. Thank you Fraulein.

The Actress, now carrying some books and magazines, crosses to Mrs Manahan

Actress Good afternoon, my dear. I've brought you some books. Biographies. I believe you like biographies . . .
Mrs Manahan Thank you, Fraulein Hoede.
Actress Disraeli. He was a British Prime Minister.

Mrs Manahan I know. A great favourite of Queen Victoria.... What's this?
Actress Very interesting—and very long. A biography of Bismarck ... I found it fascinating, but then my father was in the Consular Service. He was all over the place, particularly in Yalta.

The Actress now starts to speak in Russian—I have put here the English translation of what they say but if possible Russian should be spoken

I used to love walking in the parks there ... Lyetam ani krassivie. A—zimoy luche.
Mrs Manahan (*in Russian*) They are lovely. In a way, though, I preferred the parks in St Petersburg. I'll take this book on Bismarck.
Actress Of course. You don't want any others?
Mrs Manahan Niet.

The Actress moves away

(*Watching her suspiciously*) Oh, God. I was speaking Russian. They are trying to trap me. I have no friends. No friends at all. Even when nice, they aren't my friends. That's what I must remember always ...

The Actress crosses to the Inspector and the Actor

Actress She talks Russian like a native.
Inspector So that's what her accent is.
Actress She gives certain words the harsh Russian stress in the first syllable. It was silly of me not to have realized it before.
Actor Thank you, Fraulein. That was most helpful.
Actress Anything to help.

The Actress exits

Inspector Have you questioned her about her childhood, Doctor?
Actor Yes. She evades answering. Sometimes she lets things slip by accident, but a direct question shuts her up.
Inspector Her arm still hurts her, I suppose?
Actor Yes. It's better, but I'm sure still painful at times.
Inspector Is she pretending?
Actor I'm sure she's not. We've had her here for two years. No one can keep up a pretence like that for that time. She's unquestionably well-educated. In several languages too. German, English and now Russian. Her choice of words is felicitous. She's been surrounded by erudite, articulate people all her life. Shall I tell you what I think?

The Actress enters, picks up a shawl and again looks quite different. She crosses the stage and sits in a chair

She's suffering from auto suggestive amnesia which is perfectly genuine but which originates in the wish to suppress unpleasant experiences. She has a basically happy nature, and so when she's happy and relaxed this comes out and she can unconsciously mention the past, but only happy memories. The moment she's questioned and she thinks consciously about the past, she retreats and withdraws and forgets. It's a defence mechanism at work.

Inspector Can we break it down?

Actor Very difficult. A shock or an extreme emotion like sudden blind rage could do it perhaps.

They exit

Mrs Manahan sees the Actress as Klara Peuthert seated, crosses to her and smiles pleasantly

Mrs Manahan You're the new patient here?

The Actress is silent and looks at her

I'm one of the patients too. It's a bit frightening when you first come here, isn't it? But you'll get used to it.

The Actress is suspicious and stares at her. Mrs Manahan is kind and pleasant and warm and friendly

I've been here two years now and so I often help the nurses.

The Actress is silent and stares

Would you like something to read? These magazines are nice.

Silence. Mrs Manahan moves away. The Actress never takes her eyes off her

Why is she staring at me? She's done nothing else but stare at me for days. What is the matter with her? She never stares at anybody else like that. Only at me. (*She crosses the stage briskly*)

The Actress continues to stare at her

(*Stopping*) It's uncanny. Abnormal. Of course, she can't be fully sane if she's here, but why pick on me? What have I done?

Mrs Manahan, who has behaved normally and reasonably until then, suddenly becomes frightened and suspicious

She's an informer. An agent provocateur! She's a police spy! Of course! They realize I'm Russian and they're going to deport me.

Mrs Manahan starts to move agitatedly about. She sits, she gets up, she crosses and recrosses the stage. All the time the Actress stares at her. From being normal and sane, Mrs Manahan is on the verge of hysterics. Suddenly the Actress starts to shout triumphantly

Actress I've got it. It's been puzzling me for weeks but I've got it. I know you.

Mrs Manahan stares at her terrified. The Actress leaps up

I know who you are.

Mrs Manahan cringes in horror and hides her face. The Actress stands over her still shouting

I know exactly who you are. You can't fool me. (*She is jubilant and runs about the stage*) I know who she is, I know who she is.

The Actress dashes from the stage

The effect on Mrs Manahan is devastating. She is petrified and talks hysterically to herself

Mrs Manahan I admit nothing. I've never seen her before. I don't speak Russian. I'm not Russian. Not Russian. Not Russian. I can't remember anything.

The Actor runs on

Actor What the bloody hell is going on?
Mrs Manahan I know nothing. I know nothing. I know nothing. (*She starts to scream*) Oh, God help me. Help me. (*She is yelling, screaming, sobbing*)

The Inspector rushes on

Actor (*shouting*) Hold her arm.

The Inspector tries to. Mrs Manahan is struggling furiously

Inspector It's all right. No one will hurt you.
Actor Hold her arm still for me. (*He gives her an injection*)

Mrs Manahan subsides, moaning, to the floor

Find the nurse. I'll get her into bed.
Inspector Nurse! Nurse!

The Actor helps Mrs Manahan into bed

The Actress appears on the other side of the stage. She is in a state of great excitement

Actress I recognized her! I recognized her at once. Oh, she couldn't fool me. It had been worrying me for days, for weeks even. She's fooled everyone else—doctors, nurses, everyone. But not me. They say she even fooled the police. But she didn't fool me. The moment I saw her—the very moment I saw her—I said to myself, "I've seen you before". Of course I never said it out loud. That's where I was so clever. I watched her. I watched the way she walked and talked, and even the way she sat, and suddenly—bang! I recognized her. Just like that!

The telephone rings

Inspector Hallo. No, we have not found Klara Peuthert. Yes. Klara Peuthert. Yes that's right. She was a governess with the Demidoff family. Yes, in Russia. I know the Press is very interested but I don't know anything more. I'm very busy. Goodbye.

The Actor and Actress (both looking quite different from before) see each other, exclaim with delight and approach each other like old friends who haven't seen each other for years

Actor as General Countess! Is it really you?
Actress as Countess General! After all these years!
Actor (*kissing her hand*) When did we last meet?
Actress At the French Embassy, wasn't it? They gave a dinner party. You had just married.
Actor Ah, yes. We little thought . . .
Actress She escaped too, I hope?
Actor Alas, no. She was murdered with my parents in Moscow.
Actress It's too sad. So few escaped.
Actor You've heard the news?
Actress Who hasn't? Berlin talks of nothing else.
Actor Apparently it was all most dramatic. They were in the same hospital ward.
Actress Hospital? I heard they met in prison.
Actor No, it was in hospital, and this lady's maid—who's a patient—saw her, recognized her, screamed her name and fainted dead away for ten hours.

The Inspector is at his desk, talking into the telephone

Inspector Hallo. Now look here. The moment I know anything more I'll tell you. No, there is no warrant for Klara Peuthert's arrest. She is not a criminal. No, she has not been certified. Klara Peuthert was a voluntary patient and was within her rights to leave whenever she liked. Look! If you want the law changed, get on to the Minister of Health, but don't bother me. (*He rings off*) Bloody reporters!

The Actor and Actress greet each other again

Actor as Baron Madame.
Actress as Madame My dear Baron.
Actor What's the latest?
Actress I'm told they recognized each other at once.
Actor That's what the police say—but it's not true.
Actress Not true?
Actor It's a put-up job.
Actress Really?
Actor Oh yes. This lady's maid had a criminal record, and under cross-examination she confessed . . .
Actress Goodness!
Actor She's an imposter! It's absolutely true, so now they've both been arrested. There won't be a trial, of course, the authorities don't want one—in any case, she's mad.

They exit

Inspector (*on the telephone*) Put me through to extension three-nine-three, please. . . . Yes, the Foreign Department. . . . It's beginning to fit. It really is beginning to fit . . . speaks German, English, Russian, Papa had a yacht. Is Greek Orthodox, was very rich and is interested in politics. . . . Hallo. . . . It's the police here. . . . Now that is interesting. . . . When she left the

Demidoffs she worked for a while with the German Ambassador's family in St Petersburg. ... As a matter of interest, his children would be received everywhere, wouldn't they? Meet everyone? The governess, going along too as chaperon, would meet them too, wouldn't she?

The Actress enters as Sister

Well, thank you very much. You have been most helpful. Goodbye. (*He rings off*) Forgive me, Sister, and thank you for coming. Now, Sister, you are usually on duty in the daytime?

Actress Yes, Inspector, but I've told you everything I know already.

Inspector Yes, yes. We know what happens when she gets upset or excited, but you observe her all the time, don't you?

Actress That's part of my job.

Inspector What does she do when she thinks she's alone, when she thinks she's unobserved?

Actress I don't know how to answer that, where to begin.

Inspector Go through her day.

Actress The whole day?

Inspector Yes. Omit nothing.

Actress Well ... she gets up and washes, she's very clean and is quite meticulous. Many of the more disturbed patients aren't. Then she makes her bed. We encourage our patients to do little tasks like that. Most of them are slapdash about it. She isn't. She makes her bed beautifully, turns the mattress regularly, folds the sheets tidily. Come to think of it, I wouldn't be at all surprised if she'd had a little training as a nurse herself. Is anything the matter, Inspector?

The Inspector hands her a book

(*Looking at it*) Good heavens! You don't mean those wild stories we're hearing could be true?

Inspector If they're right, that is a picture of her mother in nurse's uniform. Read what it says underneath.

Actress Photograph taken at the front.

Inspector The last sentence. Read the last sentence.

Actress She always encouraged her daughters to train as nurses too. (*She cannot keep the excitement out of her voice. She loses her professional calm*) Oh, my goodness! Well! And there's even a resemblance.

Inspector Keep calm, Sister.

Actress Yes, yes, of course. I am calm, quite calm. But isn't it exciting?

Inspector It's not certain yet.

Actress (*her excitement mounting*) When she helps us with the trays, she lays them out professionally, even to the knives and forks. Why didn't we realize it before? I remember in the war I had young trainee nurses and one of the best turned out to be—well, I forget who exactly, but of most exalted birth. Oh what a to-do! What excitement! Wait till I tell them in the hospital. They'll all be so thrilled.

Inspector Don't jump to conclusions.

Actress No, no, of course not. I won't say a word.

She rushes out

Inspector Come back, Sister. It's not proved yet. Who would have thought it? Under all that professional calm, there's a silly gossipy woman trying to get out. Well, the cat's well and truly out of the bag now.

The Actor comes on

Yes, what is it constable?

Actor as Constable A Baroness Buxhoeveden and General Epatiev to see you.

Inspector Well, show them in.

The Actress enters in a hat and fur coat

The Actor puts on a monocle and picks up an elegant walking-stick

Actor as General Epatiev Inspector?

Inspector Do come in, sir. Please sit down, Madame, General.

Actor I prefer to stand, thank you.

Actress as Baroness Buxhoeveden You are doubtless aware of the extraordinary rumours sweeping Berlin.

Inspector Indeed.

Actor In all probability they are nonsense.

Inspector Not necessarily.

Actress This scullery maid who recognized her ...

Inspector Not a scullery maid. A governess. A German governess from a perfectly respectable middle class German family.

Actress But mad of course.

Inspector Not even that. Suffering from nervous strain.

Actor Who was she governess to?

Inspector A Sonia Demidoff.

Actress They wouldn't know anything. The countess was an invalid and never went about.

Inspector And also to the German Ambassador's daughter.

Actor (*impressed*) Oh, really.

Actress The diplomatic corps was quite separate, you know.

Inspector The rumours are very persistent.

Actor Quite so. And that is why it was felt by certain people in high places—need I say more?

Inspector No, sir.

Actor —that perhaps the matter should be investigated.

Inspector May I ask, did you know the family well?

Actress Intimately. I was her mother's closest friend. If the girl is who she claims to be ...

Inspector You must understand the position. She doesn't claim anything. For over three years she has refused to answer any questions about her past. This governess declares she recognized her, and that started the rumours. No one can stop her talking.

Actress I suppose we must see her, but it's all very unsatisfactory. Two lunatics in an asylum concoct a preposterous story ...

Inspector They are not lunatics. They were in the asylum for observation. One has quite legally discharged herself and the other has nowhere to go. Whilst certainly very ill with a tubercular arm, she has not been certified insane nor does any doctor believe her mad. In view of the rumours, the authorities decided that arrangements should be made for friends of her family to see her—but I beg of you both—go with open minds. Will you come this way, please?

They cross to Mrs Manahan who is staring apathetically into space. The Actor and Actress look at her in dismay

Actress What is your name?

Silence

Actor Where were you born?

Silence

Do you recognize me? (*He turns to the Inspector*) If she's not mad what is wrong with her? I mean she can't be genuine. I was on duty every day. If she doesn't remember me she won't remember anyone.

Actress What happened when we were all arrested? You see she doesn't answer. It's ridiculous. Her mother was devoted to me.

Actor You see, Inspector, all the girls were very strictly brought up. They had manner.

Actress Poise.

Actor They were polite. They were trained to talk to strangers easily.

Actress They received people properly. I remember when the eldest girl came into society, the ease with which she made "the circle" created a sensation.

Actor Perhaps if we could see her walk about.

Inspector Would you walk for us, please?

Mrs Manahan does so

Actress Will you sit?

Mrs Manahan stops. She opens her mouth to speak, thinks better of it and sits

Actor Now smile.

Actress Well then, wave to somebody.

Mrs Manahan looks at her angrily and doesn't move

She doesn't wave. It would give her away if she did. They incline their head in an inimitable way when they wave.

They are on either side of her

Actor Who was your tutor?

Actress You maid?

Actor Have you ever had measles?

Actress Chicken pox?

Actor Pneumonia?

Actress What illness did your brother have?
Actor Who's in this photograph?
Actress Who are this group?
Actor What relation is this man to you?
Actress Where was this taken?
Actor Who's the woman in the carriage?
Mrs Manahan Grandmama.

Silence

Actor She recognized her grandmother.
Actress Oh you're so gullible, General. Any Russian peasant girl could do that. Her photograph was everywhere.
Inspector Have you reached any conclusion?
Actor It's not Tatiana, that's for sure. Too small. It could be Anastasia, I suppose.
Actress Never. It's not Anastasia. No, no, no. It's not her at all.
Mrs Manahan It, it, it. I am not it. I am Anastasia. I am the Grand Duchess Anastasia Nicolaevna, youngest daughter of Tsar Nicholas II of Russia.

Black-out except for a spot on Mrs Manahan

Voices come out of the darkness at her

Voices How old are you?
Who was your grandmother?
Do you speak French?
German?
Russian?
English?
Did you always curtsy to your parents?
Who were your mother's ladies-in-waiting?
Why didn't you speak up sooner?
How did you escape ...?

The Lights go full up

Mrs Manahan is alone with the Inspector

Mrs Manahan Stop! Stop! Stop! You must stop them, Inspector. They all come and shout at me and look at me and tell me, "Do this, do that." And then German authorities—health authorities—want me to claim a relation, any relation to get rid of me. But how can I do that?
Inspector The German health authorities have kept you at public expense for three years. They cannot be expected to do this for ever.
Mrs Manahan What can I do? I know no one.
Inspector You know me. My wife and I would be happy for you to stay with us for a while, and I will see how I can help you. There are Russians, and relations too, who are concerned for your welfare. (*He takes her arm*) We should leave the hospital, don't you think? Today—and I will drive you to my home. We live a little way out. There are woods and fields and you can convalesce.

Mrs Manahan Yes. I'd like that . . .

He sits down and reads a newspaper

She comes up to him

Inspector Have a nice walk?
Mrs Manahan It was lovely. The woods are looking beautiful. I've not been so happy for a long, long time. When will my relations visit me?
Inspector Soon, soon. It all takes time. There are all these forms.
Mrs Manahan Whatever for?
Inspector About you.
Mrs Manahan Me?
Inspector Officialdom doesn't know what to do about you, and in such a situation they send forms. It's a habit they have. I'm at the moment your guardian, so I must fill them in somehow. (*He crosses to the desk*) Will you help me?
Mrs Manahan If I can.
Inspector Good. Where were you born?
Mrs Manahan Peterhof. It's near Petersburg. My parents had a castle there.
Inspector What year?
Mrs Manahan June the fifth, nineteen-o-one.
Inspector Mother's name?
Mrs Manahan She was Empress of Russia.
Inspector Maiden name?
Mrs Manahan Princess Alix of Hesse-Darmstadt. Like me she was one of four girls. Well, there was a fifth in her case, but she died of diphtheria. It was terrible, they all caught it, even my grandmother, and she died of it.
Inspector Your grandmother died?
Mrs Manahan Yes, on December the fourteenth, which was dreadful.
Inspector Why specially?
Mrs Manahan Ah well. Grandmother was English, Queen Victoria's second daughter and her father—my great grandfather, the Prince Consort—died on a December the fourteenth too. I believe Gan Gan regarded it as a terrible date throughout her life.
Inspector Gan Gan?
Mrs Manahan She called it the dreaded fourteenth. Uncle Bertie—King Edward VII of England—he had diphtheria and typhoid and nearly died on that date as well. You see, Mama was more or less English, her mother having died when she was a girl—only five or six, I think—she was brought up by her grandmother.
Inspector Gan Gan?
Mrs Manahan That's right. In England a good deal too. Months would be spent at Osborne or Balmoral. Her sisters and cousins were always visiting us in Russia.
Inspector Until the war.
Mrs Manahan That's right. Except, it's most extraordinary, I remember Uncle Ernie visiting us at Tsarskoe in nineteen-sixteen.
Inspector Who is Uncle Ernie?

Mrs Manahan The Grand Duke of Hesse, Mama's brother. He is German, so I don't know how he managed it with the war and everything, but that's when I last saw him.
Inspector You last saw your Uncle in nineteen-sixteen?
Mrs Manahan That's right.
Inspector Nineteen-fourteen surely?
Mrs Manahan No, no. Nineteen-sixteen. I'm certain.

She exits

The Actor appears at the other side of the stage

Actor as Uncle Ernie the Grand Duke of Hesse I am of course most concerned about this so-called niece of mine. Do you think she could possibly have escaped?
Inspector (*crossing to him*) Well, that's what the girl says.
Actor Is it possible? I mean, have you read the reports—the official reports—of the massacre? With eye witness accounts? I've been looking them up today... They are horrifying.
Inspector Yes, I know.
Actor The Whites took Ekaterinburg only three days after the massacre and made a full investigation. Listen to this... a Bolshevik confessed... "The whole of the Imperial family were assembled in the room, where they were informed they were to be shot, and shortly after that the soldiers fired at them. They all fell to the ground. After this the soldiers began to make sure they were all killed—and"—listen to this—"discovered that the Grand Duchess Anastasia was still alive. She was hit on the head with a rifle butt and stabbed thirty-two times."
Inspector This girl has been hit on the head and has stab wounds.
Actor Really? Yet, you know, that's not the only eye witness report. Far from it. Where are we—a sentry, Kleschev saw it all. Here we are, "He saw the Tsar and Tsarina, all four daughters being led through the yard ... into the field ... shots were fired." Prince Lvov saw the room afterwards and said it was a pool of blood. The family was made to sit in a row, and blow after blow was inflicted on them with bayonets.
Inspector She is easily frightened and, when hysterical, collapses to the floor and tries to ward off blows.
Actor You're impressed with her?
Inspector Very much. She's consistent. I'm sure she's genuine. Soldiers when shooting in a room are not calm and these, according to reports, were drunk—there was their staff as well, maids, ladies-in-waiting and so on. It's not impossible for one victim to be severely wounded and left for dead and yet survive. It really isn't.
Actor And you say she has these terrible wounds?
Inspector Yes.
Actor You think I should see her?
Inspector I'm sure you should, Your Highness.
Actor Well perhaps... I mean I certainly don't wish to be unkind to her—but to escape that terror...

Inspector I'm sure you would believe her if you saw her. She speaks of you often, sir. She remembers when she last saw you.
Actor When was that?
Inspector In nineteen-sixteen. I suppose you were on some sort of secret mission to your sister.

There's a pause

Actor I was never in Russia in nineteen-sixteen.
Inspector What?
Actor If she says that she is clearly an imposter. Or deranged—after all you found her in an asylum. How could I, a German Ruling Prince, visit Russia when we were at war with her. It's ridiculous. If you will excuse me, I'll arrange for you to be shown out.

He exits

The Inspector stands still

Mrs Manahan comes in

Inspector I've just been to see the Grand Duke of Hesse.
Mrs Manahan Yes. Tell me.

The Inspector speaks sharply and embarks for the first time on a hostile examination

Inspector No, you tell me. When did you last see him.
Mrs Manahan Nineteen-sixteen.
Inspector Nineteen-sixteen?
Mrs Manahan Yes.
Inspector The Grand Duke denies it.
Mrs Manahan How can he when it's true?
Inspector Our two countries were at war. It would have been treasonable for a German General to secretly visit the enemy. It can't have been nineteen-sixteen.
Mrs Manahan Well, it was.
Inspector Nineteen-fourteen perhaps?
Mrs Manahan No.
Inspector You're mistaken.
Mrs Manahan I am not mistaken. I remember it so well because we were at war. It was extraordinary seeing him then.
Inspector You are lying.
Mrs Manahan I never lie.
Inspector Tell me of that night.
Mrs Manahan What night?
Inspector Of the murder.
Mrs Manahan Again? We go over and over it.
Inspector There must be some proof, some definite clue.
Mrs Manahan Why *must* be?
Inspector There always is.
Mrs Manahan There are eye witness accounts of my escape. They believe in the murders, why not my escape? Where is that report ...? "We took blankets from the other bodies and rolled her up. We put her in a cart and

rode off." There it is in black and white. Did I make that up? Why must I tell you again. Papa, Mama, my sisters and Alexis were all killed. I can still hear their screaming.

Inspector You were all asleep?

Mrs Manahan Yes, on the floor.

Inspector All of you?

Mrs Manahan No, no. Mama and Alexis were in beds.

Inspector Why Alexis?

Mrs Manahan He was ill. Haemophilia. The blood doesn't clot.

Inspector They woke you up?

Mrs Manahan Yes.

Inspector Who?

Mrs Manahan The guards.

Inspector Why?

Mrs Manahan They said there were disturbances in the town. But it wasn't true. We were taken downstairs.

Inspector To the cellar?

Mrs Manahan They call it that in the report but that's not right. It was a large room, a dining-room, I think.

Inspector On the ground floor?

Mrs Manahan Yes, yes.

Inspector Windows?

Mrs Manahan Of course.

Inspector You were in this room. Then what happened?

Mrs Manahan They began firing.

Inspector At once?

Mrs Manahan Yes.

Inspector Were you seated?

Mrs Manahan Mama had sat. Papa was holding Alexis. There was blood, blood everywhere. I tried to hide. I prayed. . . . I lost consciousness. (*She collapses, sobbing*)

The Inspector looks at her dispassionately. He walks away, waiting for her to calm down

Inspector You told me of your mother's mother. Who was your father's mother?

Mrs Manahan The Dowager Empress. She was—is—a Danish Princess.

Inspector Is?

Mrs Manahan She's still alive.

Inspector (*rounding on her suddenly*) After you were rolled up in the blankets and put into the cart, what happened?

She stares at him blankly for a moment

Mrs Manahan You're a nice man, but you're like everyone else. You will ask questions, questions all the time. What happened and what do I remember? I only know what I was told by my rescuers. They were peasants, Polish peasants. I remember the pain and the darkness and the fear. My hair was sticky with blood. The cart was shaking and I kept screaming. And I remember voices, strange voices, talking urgently to me.

I remember lying in straw and hands, rough hands, trying to comfort me. How long this torment lasted I don't know. We were all hungry and thirsty. I remember calling out for food.

Inspector We. How many were you?

Mrs Manahan There were four of them. Two men and two women. Their name was Tchaikowsky. One was called Alexander. They spoke Russian to me, but Polish to each other . . .

Inspector So they got you out of Russia?

Mrs Manahan Yes, to Romania.

Inspector The Queen of Romania. She is your aunt?

Mrs Manahan More or less. Cousin to both my parents.

Inspector Why didn't you go to her?

Mrs Manahan I was pregnant.

Inspector When? How?

Mrs Manahan How do I know? I was unconscious most of the time, in pain. I would cry all night. It was cold, always cold. Alexander would comfort me. When I understood what had happened to me, I insisted on marrying him.

Inspector How did you insist?

Mrs Manahan I made scenes, threatened to kill myself, so he gave way and married me.

Inspector Where?

Mrs Manahan A church in Bucharest.

Inspector What was it called?

Mrs Manahan I don't know. All I remember is a dark church and a ceremony.

Inspector What happened to the child?

Mrs Manahan It was a son. I don't want to talk about it. My husband was killed in Bucharest. That's what I was told. I don't KNOW anything.

Inspector How were you living?

Mrs Manahan On the jewels.

Inspector Jewels?

Mrs Manahan Jewellery was sewn into my clothes by Mama. We sold them all.

Inspector Why did you go to Berlin?

Mrs Manahan To get help.

Inspector Who from?

Mrs Manahan My Aunt Irene, Princess Henry of Prussia, my mother's sister. That was another terrible journey. We travelled by night.

Inspector Why?

Mrs Manahan We had no papers.

Inspector You walked to Berlin?

Mrs Manahan No, no. We crossed frontiers on foot by night—once across the frontier, we went by train—terrible carriages packed with people.

Inspector Who's we?

Mrs Manahan My brother-in-law and myself.

Inspector Why did he come along?

Mrs Manahan They needed money too. They couldn't get work. There were endless discussions. Finally it was decided that my mother-in-law would look after the child, and my brother-in-law and I would go to Berlin. Why do you make me talk about such things? The whole episode horrified me. I was ashamed. I never saw the child again.

Inspector Tell me about Berlin.

Mrs Manahan Berlin?

Inspector Yes Berlin. Why Berlin?

Mrs Manahan I told you. My aunt lived there.

Inspector Where?

Mrs Manahan I don't know. She had a palace there.

Inspector Where did you stay?

Mrs Manahan Neither of us had been to Berlin before. We found a hotel. It was terrible.

Inspector Its name?

Mrs Manahan I don't know. I don't know anything. I was ill. In a daze, frightened—I'd never been anywhere unescorted, so my brother-in-law did it all for me. We got two rooms. I went to my room to try and rest. But it was impossible. The pain in my arm. My head ached. I went to my brother-in-law's room. He had gone out. I waited and waited. Time meant nothing to me. Did I wait an hour or a day? I don't know. I decided to go out and began wandering about the streets. Suddenly I realized, with what terror I cannot tell you, that I was lost. I didn't know the name of the hotel, of the street it was in, not even the district. First of all I tried to retrace my steps ... then I got in a panic and ran and ran till I was exhausted. Suddenly I saw this water. There were trees. It was quiet and deserted. In the water lay the answer to all my problems. It would cover me, protect me, take me away. The pain would stop, the despair would end, the tiredness would be gone. I believe I was already dead as I stepped into the water ... (*she pauses and looks at him*) They say you can only die once. That's quite untrue. I have died twice already. I pray that when I die the third time, I won't return again.

The Inspector looks at her

Inspector Shall I tell you something? (*He looks at her and grins and reverts to his usual friendly manner*) I believe you. Yes, I do. I believe you absolutely as I believe my own mother. You are who you say you are.

Mrs Manahan Well, of course.

Inspector What you must do now is relax and get well. (*He takes her by the arm*) You must breathe the fresh air, go for walks and try not to worry about anything.

Mrs Manahan exits

The Inspector crosses to the desk and sits

The Actor enters

Actor as Gardener Her Royal Highness is here, sir.

The Inspector rises. He is very respectful

Inspector Show her in.
Actor Her Royal Highness Princess Henry of Prussia, sir.

The Actress comes in. She has on furs and a smart hat and gloves

Inspector Your Royal Highness. (*He kisses her hand*)
Actress as Aunt Irene, Princess Henry of Prussia Inspector . . .
Inspector I am much honoured, Your Highness, at your coming to see me. Would you care to sit down?

She sits

Actress My husband disapproves.
Inspector Oh dear.
Actress I was so much intrigued by your letter that I decided to hear what you have to say.
Inspector It's very good of you.
Actress If she's genuine, our family will be so grateful.
Inspector Oh, she's genuine all right.
Actress But how can you be so sure?
Inspector I'm a policeman, and I can tell when someone is lying or trying to pull the wool over my eyes. I have to tell you—it is my duty to tell you—that I believe her to be what she says she is, the youngest daughter of your sister, the late Tsarina. If you look at the alternatives dispassionately, there are only four worthy of serious consideration. First and foremost, she could be an imposter.
Actress Yes indeed—seven people have already claimed to be the Tsar's children—there have been four Olgas. One Alexis—miraculously recovered from haemophilia—and at least two Tatianas.
Inspector But these others have made claims and issued statements. The Grand Duchess Anastasia has done neither. Indeed she has tried to keep her identity secret. Now that for an imposter is most unusual. If she is an imposter—that is, a woman deliberately and criminally intending to assume a false identity for gain—then her way of going about it is most extraordinary. In February nineteen-twenty she is found more dead than alive in a canal. She refuses to answer questions. She has bouts of hysteria and when her identity is—after two years—guessed at, she remains unco-operative. When visited by members of her parents' court she was silent and hostile. Now an imposter tries to convince, not to alienate.
Actress Perhaps she's very cunning.
Inspector I am used to cross-examining people. She's a truthful person, I know she is. She never attempts to cover up gaps in her knowledge. And she is unshakeable after repeated questioning. She is in no sense an imposter.
Actress She could be mad.
Inspector She isn't.
Actress She was in an asylum.
Inspector For observation only.
Actress For two years?

Inspector She had nowhere else to go. The Authorities can't turn a young sick woman out into the streets. If she is mad, she has convinced every doctor she's seen that she's sane. Hysterical, yes. Difficult and peculiar, yes. But not insane.

Actress Of course I am most concerned, Inspector. I wouldn't be here if I wasn't. I pray indeed that a miracle happened and that someone did escape the massacre, but one mustn't be gullible.

Inspector She's been stabbed by bayonets. She's been hit over the head brutally—she certainly escaped a massacre somewhere. Listen to this. All the reports of the massacre single Anastasia out in a most curious fashion—"Of the Tsar's family, I remember that Anastasia was the only one mentioned as being stabbed. . . ." Or this statement—"The Grand Duchess Anastasia was still alive, she was stabbed thirty-two times," and then this one from an Austrian prisoner of war. . . . "Someone said he saw a girl's body move. We took blankets from the other bodies and rolled her up in them carefully. She screamed. I recognized her as Anastasia. We put her in a cart and rode off. We didn't go far, 200 yards, then we stopped at the house of one of the Russians and got Anastasia into a bed. . . ." The Head of the Swedish Red Cross had his train searched for a missing Grand Duchess. Now, are all those people lying? And if so why? Now, she has astonishing knowledge of Royalty. She knows relationships, backgrounds. If she isn't Anastasia, then we are presented with the question, "who is she?" The final alternative, madam, is that she is exactly who she says she is, your niece and the Tsar's daughter.

Actress What do you want me to do?

Inspector I want you to see her and talk to her.

Actress Yes. I'll do that. But on condition she is not told my name. Introduce me as Countess somebody or other. Countess Hofnoye . . .

Inspector Whoever she is, Madam, she has been through a dreadful ordeal. She is therefore strange, easily frightened, easily offended. It's ten years or so since you last saw your niece. You must expect her to be very different. Do not hope to see the carefree girl you once knew.

Mrs Manahan comes in happily. She is carrying some mushrooms

May I introduce you to the Countess Hofnoye.

Actress How do you do?

Mrs Manahan You must excuse me. I have been for such a long walk. I must go and wash at once.

Actress Oh there's no need. Sit down and talk to me. This is my first visit here. I didn't know how pretty this part of Berlin is. We live on the other side, you know. Up North we have a little place in the country. Is anything wrong? You look upset.

Mrs Manahan stares at her wildly, bursts into tears and crosses the stage

Actress (*following her*) Anastasia—is it really you? Why don't you speak to me? Do you remember me? Who am I? Tell me my name, dear.

Mrs Manahan retreats. The Actress follows

Give me a sign. I've come here to be your friend. Tell me my name, dear. I want to help you, truly.

Mrs Manahan sobs bitterly and moans

You must listen to me. Why should I come here at all if I didn't want to help you? Just tell me my name.

Mrs Manahan covers her face in her hands and sobs hysterically

That's all I ask. My name.

Mrs Manahan sobs and sobs

Give me some indication you know me and who I am. My name, Anastasia. What is my name?

Mrs Manahan gets up and still sobbing, goes from the room

Well Inspector, I am sorry. I did try.

Inspector Yes. You did.

Actress Why is she silent? Why did she go from the room? If she recognizes me, why not say my name?

Inspector Why not indeed.

Actress There is a certain resemblance, I admit, but it's certainly not strong enough for me to acknowledge her as my niece. The hair, the forehead and yes, even the eyes are Anastasia's. But the mouth and the chin are not hers at all. No, I cannot positively identify her.

Inspector So it isn't Anastasia?

Actress I didn't say that. I cannot say it is her and yet I cannot say it isn't. I wish I could give you more comfort, Inspector, but I can't.

The Actress exits

Inspector You can come back now.

Mrs Manahan returns

(*Angrily*) You didn't recognize her at all, did you?

Mrs Manahan Recognize her? Of course I recognized her. That's my Aunt Irene. Princess Henry of Prussia. How dare she come here like that? How dare she pretend to be somebody else! It's intolerable, shameful, disgusting. I'm not an exhibit to be examined, questioned, looked at. I am me, ME.

Inspector But dear God, that's what I'm trying to help you prove. That's what I've given up time and money to do. Two little words, that's all I wanted. Why couldn't you say the two words "Aunt Irene"? That's all you had to say, and then you would have won.

Mrs Manahan Won what? Am I in a competition? I don't want to win anything. I don't know what you are talking about.

Inspector We require proof.

Mrs Manahan No we don't. You may. The world may. I don't, I know who I am. That's why I've never attempted to prove anything. I answer questions. That's all. And those I answer reluctantly. In hospital when I was questioned, questioned all the time, did I answer? No, no, no. I was silent. You ask questions. I don't. Because I know the answer. I don't have to prove anything. I am who I am. That is all I have to say.

CURTAIN

ACT II

The Inspector's office

The Actress, as Grand Duchess Olga, is found alone on stage. She is seated. After a moment she gets up and looks around, crosses to the desk, sees a reference book and picks it up

The Inspector enters

Inspector Your Imperial Highness?
Actress as Grand Duchess Olga Inspector?
Inspector I'm sorry I'm late. I was working on another case.

The Actress sits

I am right, Madam? You are the Tsar's sister, the Grand Duchess Olga?
Actress Oh yes, Inspector. Some of us, at least, are quite genuine. Nor do we need reference books to find out about our families.
Inspector This is for me. Not for her. For me to check her statements and may I say, not once in all the months she's been here has she made a mistake.
Actress Does she expect me?
Inspector No. She's out for her usual walk.
Actress Princess Henry of Prussia came to see her and was not impressed. She admitted a superficial likeness, but that was all.
Inspector Madam, if you've already made up your mind that she's an imposter then this visit is pointless.
Actress But I haven't made up my mind. None of us have. I've come in the face of enormous hostility from my family, it's true, but there are so many wild stories, so many rumours. . . . We are naturally suspicious. We are not unkind, merely cautious. Princess Henry is a German Aunt, I am Russian. I saw my nieces almost every day right up to the Revolution. I really believe that no imposter will be able to fool me.

Mrs Manahan comes in. She sees the Actress and recognizes her at once

Mrs Manahan Aunt Olga.
Actress Anastasia . . .

They both burst into tears and embrace

Darling, darling. It is my little one. My brother's child. My niece come back to life.

Mrs Manahan curtsies to her and kisses her hand. Much moved the Actress raises her up and embraces her again

Mrs Manahan Oh, how glad I am to see you.
Actress Darling, darling.
Mrs Manahan I am so happy, so very happy.

They sit down together and hug each other

Actress You look pale, my darling. You must be firm with her, Inspector, and make her eat up.
Inspector I'll do my best. You'll stay to tea, will you, Ma'am?
Actress If I may.

The Inspector exits

Mrs Manahan How is Grandmama?
Actress Oh darling, she's getting old and then she has a weak heart.
Mrs Manahan I do so want to see her.
Actress And you will, I promise you. Soon darling, soon.
Mrs Manahan Do you remember when Grandmama came to my last birthday party at Tsarskoe Selo . . . we played blind man's bluff and I fell over and cut my knee: and I cried—and Grandmama said, "Romanovs never cry"?
Actress Oh my darling, I do remember. I think of the old days all the time, how happy they were. And now your old Aunt has found you again, she will never forsake you. Never. When you leave here, I will see what I can do to help. You cannot go on living with no money and on charity from that nice Inspector. I wonder if Uncle Vladimir could help. You mustn't be a cry-baby. You always were. We must be practical. Why are you laughing.
Mrs Manahan That's what you always said, "We must be practical."
Actress And I'm right.
Mrs Manahan Why can't I go to a bank?
Actress Well, they don't give people money just for the asking. You'll have to learn to manage as I did. Money has to be put into the bank first.
Mrs Manahan Papa did.
Actress Did what, dear?
Mrs Manahan Put money in the bank.
Actress What bank?
Mrs Manahan The Bank of England, I think.
Actress How—how much money?
Mrs Manahan Twenty million roubles.
Actress Twenty million?
Mrs Manahan Is that going to be enough?
Actress Enough?
Mrs Manahan For me to live on.
Actress I think so.
Mrs Manahan It's all in gold, I believe.
Actress Gold?
Mrs Manahan That's what Papa said.
Actress Oh, my goodness!
Mrs Manahan What's the matter?

Actress It's getting late. I had no idea of the time. I must go I'm afraid.
Mrs Manahan Oh, so soon?
Actress I must get back to Copenhagen. The family will want to know all about you. Make my excuses to the Inspector, there's a good girl.
Mrs Manahan But you must stay. He'll be so disappointed and so will I. I'll hurry him up.

Mrs Manahan exits quickly

The Inspector enters

Inspector Must you really go, madam?
Actress I'm afraid so, or I shall miss my train.
Inspector Well?
Actress I'm not sure. There is a certain similarity but it's not as strong as all that.
Inspector But you recognized her. I saw how you greeted each other. Surely you will make a statement, sign an affidavit that she is your niece.
Actress I cannot do anything without the full approval of my family. I mean I couldn't swear an oath she was my niece. Good afternoon, Inspector.

The Actress exits

Mrs Manahan enters

Mrs Manahan Where is she? Where's Aunt Olga?
Inspector Gone. What happened? Something must have happened.
Mrs Manahan Nothing.
Inspector Tell me exactly what was said.
Mrs Manahan We chatted away.
Inspector About what?
Mrs Manahan About how I was to live when I leave here. We talked about my birthday party. And Grandmama . . . and I said I could go to the bank.
Inspector Bank?
Mrs Manahan Yes. Papa put money in the Bank of England. Twenty million roubles. In gold.
Inspector You told her that?
Mrs Manahan Yes. It could be quite useful, couldn't it?

For a moment the Inspector cannot speak. Then he cries out in rage and anguish

Inspector Oh God! If anyone needs proof that you're the Tsar's daughter, this is it! And only I've witnessed it. Why didn't you mention the money before? And why did you have to mention it to your relations today and not to me much earlier?
Mrs Manahan I don't understand.
Inspector Let me explain. Twenty million roubles in gold is more money than anyone else has in the world—at the pre-war rate of exchange.
Mrs Manahan Exchange?

Inspector To say nothing of the interest payable on it—it must be worth even more today. Now the fact that you understood nothing of this must mean that you were brought up in a world in which money had no value at all. So your father was at the very least very very rich indeed, and could very well be the Tsar.

Mrs Manahan Well, that's all to the good, isn't it?

Inspector What isn't to the good is that by telling your relations about the money you have given them the most powerful argument never to recognize you.

Mrs Manahan I didn't think it important.

Inspector What did your Aunt say when you told her? The exact words, if you can remember them.

Mrs Manahan She asked me how much?

Inspector You told her?

Mrs Manahan Yes.

Inspector Go on.

Mrs Manahan I asked if it was enough to live on.

Inspector What did she say?

Mrs Manahan She said, "I think so". Then she said she was in a hurry to get back to Copenhagen.

Inspector I'm sure she was. It's just as I thought. The money changes everything. Beforehand, it was merely a question of recognition. Will your family recognize you or won't they? Now it is a legal problem. The bank won't surrender a halfpenny of that money until they are certain who you are. If you are not Anastasia, then she is dead, isn't she?

Mrs Manahan Yes. I suppose so.

Inspector And if you're dead, your family will get the money. Don't you understand? They need the money. And to get it, you must be dead.

Mrs Manahan I never thought of that.

Inspector You will have to spend the rest of your life thinking of nothing else.

They exit

The Actor, as a Lawyer, enters and sits at the desk

The Actress, as a receptionist, enters

Actress as Receptionist Mrs Tchaikowsky is here, sir. Herr Guenter will see you now.

Actor as Lawyer Show her in. Will you sit down?

Mrs Manahan comes in. She is nervous and consequently not at her best

The Actress exits

Actor Mrs Tchaikowsky?

Mrs Manahan Yes.

Actor Do please sit down.

Mrs Manahan Thank you.

Actor I have been asked to represent you by the Inspector.

Mrs Manahan Yes, yes I know.
Actor You are Mrs Tchaikowsky?
Mrs Manahan Yes.
Actor When did you marry?
Mrs Manahan Sometime in nineteen-nineteen.
Actor Sometime?
Mrs Manahan I'm not sure of the date. I was ill.
Actor Is your husband still alive?
Mrs Manahan No.
Actor When did he die?
Mrs Manahan Sometime in nineteen-nineteen—also.
Actor Your parents?
Mrs Manahan But surely you know all this. The Inspector must have told you. It is all in the newspapers.
Actor As your legal adviser, I have to have all the facts from you.
Mrs Manahan I see. Very well. I was born in Peterhof on June the fifth, nineteen-o-one. My parents were the Emperor and Empress of Russia. There was a revolution. We were taken to Ekaterinburg, Siberia. Once there, all my family was murdered . . . I alone escaped . . . how, I don't know . . . a Polish family took me to Romania and from there I went to Berlin. I would say at a guess that I have answered these questions, told the same story, not less than ten thousand times. It is becoming almost as meaningless to me at the alphabet. A B C D E F G H I J K. There, I know the alphabet . . . one two three four five six seven eight nine ten. Look, I can count up to ten. I know where I was born. I know who my parents are and I know who I am.
Actor Mrs Tchaikowsky.
Mrs Manahan I don't want you as my lawyer.
Actor As you wish. I wasn't asking you questions about your life disbelieving you, nor to test you. They were questions that are put to any client. What seemed silly and unnecessary to you are just routine. Will you allow me to try again? Now, you have no doubt who you are. Nor have I. The problem facing us both is to prove it.
Mrs Manahan Why do I have to?
Actor There is the money.
Mrs Manahan I don't care about it.
Actor Others do.
Mrs Manahan Let them have it.
Actor Ah. The banks have a duty, a very real duty to protect their clients. Now your father put the money in the Bank for his daughters. They can give it only to them. That is to say, to you. But first of all, you have to prove legally who you are. I have to tell you—every single one of your close relatives has finally come out against you. Your Grandmother and your father's two sisters. Your mother's family are as hostile. More so in fact. They are saying that Anastasia died with her family and that you are a deranged woman making idiotic claims, which are transparent nonsense. We have to prove the opposite.
Mrs Manahan Grandmama too?
Actor Yes—the Dowager Empress too.

Mrs Manahan So even she has turned against me. How? Why? She has not seen me, spoken to me, never written to me. How can she know? Very well then, if they want a fight, they can have one. What do I have to do?
Actor Co-operate with your friends. You must not underestimate the case against you nor the power of your relatives. We can only help you if you will answer everything . . . submit to every test . . .
Mrs Manahan Very well. (*She crosses to another chair and sits*)

The Actor exits as she does so

The Actress enters and goes briskly to Mrs Manahan

Actress as Receptionist Would you step this way, please. Sit down, please. Quite still now.

Mrs Manahan obeys

The left profile first.

The Actor comes in with a camera. He takes a photograph

Now the right side.

The Actor photographs the right side

In the photograph of the Grand Duchess as a child, the ears are distinctive. Can we photograph the ears? If you would put back your hair, please? That's all. Thank you very much.

The Actor moves in to take a close up of her ears

Mrs Manahan crosses to another chair

The Actor and Actress move in to her

Actress Name?
Mrs Manahan Anastasia Nicolaevna.
Actress Age? Date of birth?
Mrs Manahan Twenty-one. June fifth, nineteen-o-one.
Actress Date of last dental treatment?
Mrs Manahan Some time in nineteen-sixteen.
Actor as Dentist Open your mouth, please.

Mrs Manahan obeys

Yes. Good dental treatment. Gold filling at fourth back molar.
Actress Anastasia's was at fifth back.
Actor Yes, yes, that's it one, two, three, four, yes, fifth. One tooth slightly broken, the third.
Actress Yes, that's right . . . fits in entirely with her dentist's report . . .
Mrs Manahan He escaped?
Actor Yes, indeed.
Mrs Manahan Oh, he was such a nice man. He'd make me laugh. Where is he living now?
Actor Lausanne, I think.
Actress Would you come over here, please.

Mrs Manahan crosses to another chair

The Actor kneels and looks at her feet

Actress Treatment for bunion. Mild surgical treatment. Local anaesthetic, I expect.
Mrs Manahan I was a difficult patient and had a general anaesthetic.
Actress Scar on knee. You fell?
Mrs Manahan That's right. On my birthday.

Mrs Manahan crosses to the desk as does the Actor

Actor Who is Missy?
Mrs Manahan Queen of Romania.
Actor Ducky?
Mrs Manahan Her sister.
Actor Who is the Grand Duke Michael?
Mrs Manahan Which one?
Actor Which one?
Mrs Manahan There are several. Three at any rate. There's my Uncle, the Grand Duke Michael Alexandrovich—there's my father's great Uncle, son of Tsar Nicholas I. And then there's his son, the Grand Duke Michael Michaelovich.
Actor Did you always curtsy to your parents?
Mrs Manahan Morning and evening, when we greeted them and on saying good-night. And of course on special occasions.
Actor To anyone else?
Mrs Manahan To Grandmama and to all Monarchs and their wives but that's all. (*She crosses* C *stage*)
Actress (*circling round her*) What language did you speak at home?
Mrs Manahan English.
Actress Why?
Mrs Manahan My mother preferred it.
Actor (*from the desk*) Your Mother was German by birth?
Mrs Manahan That may be so. She was English by upbringing. Her governess was English.
Actress What was her name?
Mrs Manahan Mrs Jackson. English was my mother's first language.
Actress Did you speak German?
Mrs Manahan Of course.
Actress And Russian?
Mrs Manahan Naturally.
Actor To whom?
Mrs Manahan To Papa, of course. And usually to the servants.
Actress How do you account for your tutor saying you spoke no German as a child?
Mrs Manahan I can't account for it at all. He's mistaken.
Actress He testified in court that you spoke no German.
Mrs Manahan Then he's lying . . . we all spoke German—the English Royal Family speaks German, and so do we.

Actor Why don't you speak Russian?
Mrs Manahan I do.
Actor When anyone talks to you in Russian you answer in German.
Mrs Manahan I dislike speaking it. It makes me unhappy. Why should I speak it if I don't want to?
Actress You persist in stating the Grand Duke of Hesse went to Russia in nineteen-sixteen.
Mrs Manahan I do.
Actress He denies it.
Actor His staff denies it.
Actress His sisters deny it.
Actor The whole world says you are wrong.
Mrs Manahan I can't help that. I am right.
Actor The money.
Mrs Manahan Again.
Actress How much money?
Mrs Manahan Twenty million roubles.
Actor In gold?
Mrs Manahan That's right.
Actress Your family says there is no money.
Mrs Manahan Then why are they contesting my claim?
Actor They deny its existence.
Mrs Manahan Once my identity is proved, then the Banks will have to hand over any money to me and we will know who is right.
Actor But they will never do that.
Mrs Manahan Why not?
Actor It would ruin them. Twenty million roubles in gold at pre-war rate of exchange would be an incalculable sum in English money, two hundred million pounds at least—to say nothing of the interest accruing from all this money. A thousand million at a guess. Therefore, the Bank will finance any and every effort to stop you collecting and to stop your relations collecting too. They in fact want the dispute to go on for ever.
Mrs Manahan It is not the money I am after. It is the establishment of my identity.
Actor You cannot do one without the other. She's mad.
Actress Found in an asylum.
Actor What money?
Actress There's no money.
Actor Her ears are different.
Actress Her teeth the same.
Actor Which bank?
Actress Who's Missy?
Actor Baby Bee.
Actress Who's Sandro . . .? Who did Aunt Louise marry?
Actor Who is Uncle Affie?
Actress Explain the Coburg Inheritance.
Actor Money, money.
Actress She's after money.

Mrs Manahan Money, money, money. All anyone wants is money . . . (*She starts to scream. Once started, she can't stop. She collapses on to the floor sobbing*)

The Actor and Actress exit

The Inspector comes in. He kneels beside her

Mrs Manahan sobs bitterly, but with more restraint

Inspector I've arranged for you to stay with some people in the country where you can rest and be happy. You must not worry about money. Various relations who do believe in you are helping. (*He gets her up*)

Mrs Manahan stops sobbing and allows herself to be led to a chair

It's very peaceful and you will be left alone.
Mrs Manahan Yes, it's lovely here.

Once he's got her seated he crosses to the desk and sits and starts sorting papers

On the other side of the stage Mrs Manahan sleeps

The Actress bustles in and goes up to her

The Actor enters in a white coat

Actress She's sleeping, doctor. Shall I wake her?
Actor as Doctor C No, let her be. Can I see her temperature chart? Oh good. How has she been?

Mrs Manahan stirs restlessly

Actress as Landlady A bit better, I think.
Mrs Manahan (*calling out in her sleep*) Niet, Niet, Niet. (*In Russian*) Awi nass ubiyut.
Actress What's she saying?
Actor I don't know. It's Russian. I think she often calls out in her sleep.
Mrs Manahan Mama, papa. (*She jabbers unintelligibly, then continues in Russian*) Awi nass abiyut. Awi nass ubiyut. Awi nass ubiyut. (*She gives one scream and collapses*)

The Actress crosses to her and starts to mop her brow and make her more comfortable

Actor Don't wake her. But once she is awake, sponge her down, and give her a little light gruel and plenty of fluids. Orange juice, water, tea, anything she wants.
Actress Yes, doctor.

They exit

The Lights go right down

Mrs Manahan (*calling in a high childish voice*) Mama, Mama. Can I play with Alexis?

The Lights go up. Mrs Manahan is asleep

(*In her sleep*) Let's race, Alexis. I can run faster than you—(*She screams*) Alexis's fallen. Mama, Mama, Alexis's fallen.

The Actress rushes in

Mrs Manahan wakes up, starts to sob and clings to the Actress

Actress (*comforting her*) We had a horrid nightmare, didn't we?
Mrs Manahan Yes.
Actress You were saying something about Alexis . . .
Mrs Manahan I was racing with him. He fell.
Actress Alexis's fallen. Yes, that's what you said. Of course it was English so I couldn't quite understand it.
Mrs Manahan Yes, we always spoke English at home, you see.

The Actor, still in his white coat, enters and crosses to the Inspector

Actor She never makes a mistake.
Inspector Never.
Actor How can she possibly be an imposter or mad?
Inspector The family are implacably hostile.
Actor Well, they would be.
Inspector Because of the money.
Actor No, no, Inspector, despite the fact that there have been human beings on the earth for millions of years, the science of human behaviour is in its infancy. We are constantly asked why she won't speak Russian in ordinary conversation. She understands it. She can be tricked into speaking it, she does speak it in delirium. I think she won't speak Russian in normal life because she connects Russian with an unpleasant experience, and they—her relations—reject her for precisely the same reason. She reminds them of events they have to reject and must forget. In both instances we are dealing with a mental block. On the one hand we have a woman who saw her family killed in front of her—by Russians. And this was done after two years ill-treatment—by Russians. She crossed a continent being hunted by Russians. So she rejects Russia and she will never consciously speak Russian again. On the other hand we have relations who have had their relatives all killed, their social background derided, their fortunes lost, their thrones collapse, their whole world destroyed. The survivors are in a state of deep shock and like all people in such a state they want to remove the experience from their minds. They want to forget. This woman, Mrs Tchaikowsky, Anastasia, reminds them. So they deny her existence.
Inspector They say she bears no resemblance to Anastasia.
Actor She probably doesn't. The first seventeen years of her life were secure and happy and luxurious. She was probably young for her age. In the second place, the next ten years were years of grim hardship and shock with wounds and illness—so time has ravaged her. On top of which the heavy drug treatment she's had would by itself alter her features beyond recognition.

Inspector You don't have to convince me. It's them. It's the Courts. and all this is costing money.
Actor Put me, put Fraulein Kestler in Court and we can only win . . .

The Actor exits

Actress (*butting in*) She's unquestionably genuine. I've been with her for a year now, and everything, everything persuades me she's genuine. Now she's better, of course, we go out, and once, Inspector, we went to a film.

Mrs Manahan sits up excitedly

I shall never forget it. Never, never. The film was called "The Tsar's Courier."
Mrs Manahan The Cossacks didn't have hats like that. Quite wrong. The snow is good. I went through snow like that often. (*She pauses and watches silently*) Oh, look, look, look, look. We wore dresses just like that. Only at Court of course. Did you see that? He turned his back on the Tsar. No one would ever do that. Ridiculous. Who's that? Oh it can't be! It's meant to be Grandmama when young. (*She laughs happily*) She'd never wear a dress like that, never. Oh, I like this. Excellent. The horses would come into a square just like that. Who's that group over there? Good heavens! (*She laughs*) It's meant to be the Imperial Family!! Oh dear me no, we'd never be grouped like that. Never.
Inspector Did she know you were watching?
Actress She ignored me entirely. She was completely natural. The whole cinema watched her amazed. She never noticed it.

The Actress exits

The Inspector crosses to Mrs Manahan. He kisses her hand. He greets her respectfully and with affection

Inspector Your Highness.
Mrs Manahan Inspector. You are losing your detachment.
Inspector For me you will always be the Grand Duchess Anastasia.
Mrs Manahan And for me you will always be my closest friend, my most loyal ally.
Inspector Do you know a Mrs Leeds?
Mrs Manahan No . . . I don't know of a Mrs Leeds.
Inspector Xenia Georgievna.
Mrs Manahan Oh yes, Xenia. I knew her very well. They were in England when war was declared, so they missed the Revolution.
Inspector She married an American millionaire.
Mrs Manahan Goodness!
Inspector I have been in correspondence with her. She has invited you—at her expense—to America to visit her.
Mrs Manahan Why on earth should I go?
Inspector Well, she's a cousin. She says she knows you well.
Mrs Manahan Very well. We played together often as children, but it's been fifteen, sixteen years.

Inspector She is rich. If she comes out in support of you, you will have a powerful ally. The plan is—if you agree—for you to go to Paris, where you will meet various Russians—and then go to America from Cherbourg. I will escort you to Paris and Cherbourg and then it will be goodbye. I think you should go. It's a chance not to be missed.

Mrs Manahan Goodbye. (*She stands up and extends both her hands to him*)

The Inspector kisses them, bows and exits

Mrs Manahan stands still

The Actress comes in. She has on a fur hat—in a Russian style—and furs. She takes them off

Actress as Xenia My dear!

Mrs Manahan Xenia.

Actress Oh, I'd know you anywhere.

Mrs Manahan So . . .

Actress You had a good crossing?

Mrs Manahan Excellent, thank you.

Actress Now you are not to worry about a thing, NOT a thing. When you get to our little place in Long Island, you will adore it . . . absolutely adore it.

Mrs Manahan I can't believe I've been in America for six weeks.

Actress Yes, time has flown. It's just like the old days.

She leads Mrs Manahan to a chair and they both sit. They giggle happily

Mrs Manahan Do you remember—it must have been in nineteen-twelve or thirteen, Christmas nineteen-twelve, Alexis was recovering from that terrible bout of illness he had in Poland? Well, we were all so happy that Christmas we had a particularly joyous time.

Actress Yes, of course I remember.

Mrs Manahan You, me, Nina and Marie, I think, crept up behind one of the footmen—Boris wasn't it—and as he was serving our Mama's tea, we tickled him and he dropped the tray and your Mother was furious and mine got the giggles.

Actress We had to go without pudding at supper.

Mrs Manahan But I crept into the kitchen and stole some for us all.

They laugh happily like two schoolgirls

Actress Oh yes, I'll never forget. Oh, it will be so marvellous when you are recognized by all the family—I'm doing all I can, interviewing the press, writing to relations. Listen to this. (*She crosses to the desk and reads what she's written*) And so, my dear aunt, I simply cannot escape the conclusion that it is indeed Anastasia. We talk all the time in English. Every day she reveals intimate knowledge of our family. When I come to see you in Copenhagen soon, I'm sure you will agree that I am right. (*She crosses to a chair and sits*)

The Actor comes in. He crosses to her

Actor as Reporter Mrs Leeds?
Actress Yes.
Actor I am from the *New York Times*.
Actress Oh yes.
Actor You have Mrs Tchaikowsky staying with you?
Actress Yes.
Actor And what do you think of her, Mrs Leeds?
Actress I have not the slightest doubt as to her identity and am willing to stake all my money to prove it. In all her conversations, she shows a knowledge of things and people which only Anastasia would have. I should mention especially her extraordinary familiarity with the history of the Romanovs.

The Actor exits

Mrs Manahan So you will sign an affidavit?
Actress Well, of course, darling.
Mrs Manahan Good.
Actress Just as soon as the family agrees.
Mrs Manahan But they won't agree.
Actress Nonsense. I'm in touch with them.
Mrs Manahan Why don't we go to Europe and tackle them together?
Actress That would be premature.
Mrs Manahan In what way?
Actress There is great anxiety about this money. They're writing to me all the time. I am trying to work out a compromise.
Mrs Manahan Compromise?
Actress My husband agrees. It would be best.
Mrs Manahan How?
Actress Well, you see the Banks are so tiresome—they say, prove that you are Anastasia.
Mrs Manahan With your help I can.
Actress But the Aunts, the relations say you aren't . . . and no, no, let me finish—the Banks won't pay out the money to our relations, because they say you claim it. Well, if you would withdraw your claim, then it's a pure legal fiction. The Banks will pay out the money to our relations, who in turn will give you an allowance of ten thousand pounds a year. You will be a rich woman. You see, we'll never get all the money out of the Banks, but we might be able to get part of it this way.
Mrs Manahan No. That would be virtually saying I am a liar, fraudulent. I won't do that. No, no, no.
Actress It would be an arrangement.
Mrs Manahan How dare you come to me with such a proposition! You know who I am. You will swear an affidavit. You said you would.
Actress The family must agree.
Mrs Manahan The family will never agree.
Actress My husband says I must co-operate with my family. My mother is most upset . . . I can't do it . . . They say you will be financially secure.
Mrs Manahan No, no, no, no . . . send me back to Europe.

Actress I'll go with you the moment I return from Jamaica.
Mrs Manahan Why are you going there?
Actress My husband has business there. I must go with him. Now I've arranged for you to stay with some sweet American friends. The Jennings. They're fabulously wealthy and my oldest friends in New York.

The Actress exits

The Actor comes in as Mr Jennings. He greets Mrs Manahan

Actor as Mr Jennings Good morning.
Mrs Manahan Good morning.
Actor Have you seen the papers?
Mrs Manahan No.
Actor Xenia will be so upset.
Mrs Manahan Why?
Actor She begged them not to do it, to give her more time to coax you.
Mrs Manahan Coax me to do what?
Actor To accept the arrangement.
Mrs Manahan No. I do not discuss it.
Actor Well, your relations have fired the first salvo. . . . Where are we . . .? "Mrs Tchaikowsky, at the moment in New York, who claims to be our dear niece and cousin, Anastasia Nicolaevna, daughter of the late Tsar, is not recognized by us as such. She has been visited by many members of our family, all of whom failed to discover a solitary point of resemblance." Here, read it for yourself.

Mrs Manahan rises, walks about and then turns and faces him

Mrs Manahan I wish to see a lawyer.
Actor Is that wise?
Mrs Manahan I wish to issue a statement.

The Actor crosses to the desk and sits putting on his glasses

Actor as American Lawyer What is it you wish to say?
Mrs Manahan I, the Grand Duchess Anastasia, youngest daughter . . .
Actor You should add, "and sole surviving child".
Mrs Manahan And sole surviving child . . . of the late Emperor Nicholas II of Russia declares herewith that in Ekaterinburg . . .
Actor You should insert—after our family left St Petersburg and had been banished to Ekaterinburg in Siberia.
Mrs Manahan Very well—my father informed me and my three sisters that he had deposited five million roubles each for the four of us in the Bank of England.

The Actress comes in as Mrs Jennings. She now talks in a broad American accent

Actress as Mrs Jennings I do think you are a little previous.
Mrs Manahan I'm sorry.
Actress Xenia will be most upset and she's done so much to help you.

Mrs Manahan I am most upset. Why hasn't she returned yet?
Actress Her husband had to go on to Mexico. She went with him. Xenia has other responsibilities besides you, you know. And we are left here to face the press and reporters never stop calling up.
Actor as Mr Jennings You should form a consortium.
Mrs Manahan What's that?
Actress A syndicate?
Mrs Manahan Why?
Actress Law suits are expensive. We can't afford it.
Actor Nor can Xenia.

Mrs Manahan sits. She is bewildered

Mrs Manahan How will I pay?
Actor The syndicate will advance you money.
Mrs Manahan What for?
Actress Don't be dumb. For shares.
Mrs Manahan Shares? What are shares? I don't understand.
Actor In your fortune. People buy shares in a business. In this case they will be buying shares in your fortune. You see when you get the ten thousand millions your father . . .
Mrs Manahan Twenty.
Actor Twenty thousand millions your old man deposited, you will pay out the shares.
Actress It's perfectly legal.
Mrs Manahan Oh, I see.
Actress Shares.
Actor Money.
Actress The syndicate.
Actor A company is formed.
Actress It's all quite simple.
Actor The lawyer's bill is already at fifty thousand dollars.
Mrs Manahan I don't understand. How?
Actress Item one, cable to London making claim. Item two, retaining London barrister. Item three, advancing money for accommodation.
Actor You can't live for ever on charity.
Actress Item four . . .
Actor Sign here, and here, and here.

Mrs Manahan signs some papers blindly

Actress We are giving a party.
Actor To a few dear friends.
Actress Just five hundred people.
Actor We're going to introduce you to everybody . . .
Mrs Manahan No.
Actress It'll be a sensation. They can hardly wait to see you.
Mrs Manahan No, no, no, no. I won't meet anyone, tell them to go away.
Actress But, my dear . . .

The Actor puts on a white coat during the next speech

Mrs Manahan Go away, you horrid vulgar old woman. Go away. I am not an exhibit. I am not a freak. I won't see a soul. I want to be left alone. Alone do you hear, alone, alone . . . I must be left alone.
Actress (*turning to the Actor*) My dear Doctor, we planned this party, especially for her. She leapt up, was very abusive. Very. She ran into her room, locked herself in and won't come out. You must take her away from here.
Mrs Manahan Go away!
Actor as Doctor D Can I come in.
Mrs Manahan No. Who are you?
Actor I'm a doctor. I wish to help you.
Mrs Manahan Go away. I'm perfectly well.
Actor You've got a bad arm, I know. If I could see it, please. You may need treatment.
Mrs Manahan Very well.
Actor (*going up to her slowly*) If you just would be seated, please. (*He offers his hand to help her to the chair*)
Mrs Manahan (*shrinking away*) No!
Actor No what? (*He gets hold of her bad arm*)

Mrs Manahan screams

Mrs Manahan Don't touch me. You think I'm frightened of you. Well, I am. But that doesn't mean I'm not going to fight back.
Actor Fight. All I want you to do is to sit . . .
Mrs Manahan Why?
Actor So that I can examine you.
Mrs Manahan And then what?
Actor Prescribe treatment. It would be best if you went to a nursing home.
Mrs Manahan Nursing home? I don't want to go to a nursing home. I want to go home to Europe.
Actor If you would come with me?
Mrs Manahan No.
Actor Come along now.

The Actress puts on a white coat during the following speech

He gets hold of Mrs Manahan's arm. She tries to break away from him but he's holding her too tightly. Suddenly she understands he's prepared to use force against her and she loses all control and kicks him. He grabs both arms. She screams and the struggle becomes intensified. He gets one arm behind her back and forces her to walk round the stage. He then releases her

Actor Come with me and be quiet.

Mrs Manahan stands glaring at them

They walk round her

Actor Be careful.
Actress as Nurse D She's violent.
Actor With serious delusions.

The Actress moves towards Mrs Manahan who hits out wildly at her

Get behind her.

Actress Yes.

Actor I'll attract her attention first. (*He waves his hands*) Cooee, cooee!

Mrs Manahan turns to him

The Actress nips behind her and gets her in an expert grip

Actor Put her in her cell. (*He moves to the desk*)

Mrs Manahan (*starting to shout*) Let me go. Let me go. I am the Grand Duchess Anastasia Nicolaevna.

Actress There, there.

Mrs Manahan Daughter of Tsar Nicholas II of Russia.

Actress Of course you are.

Mrs Manahan Descendent of Catherine the Great, Queen Victoria and William the Conqueror and Peter the Great.

The Actress lets go of her. Mrs Manahan collapses. The Actress crosses to the Actor

Actress Incurably insane.

Actor She'll have to be certified. Get the New York State Authorities on the telephone.

Actress Yes, Doctor.

Mrs Manahan crouches in her chair and lets out a howl of despair. The Actress crosses to her. She speaks gently and no longer in an American accent. The Actor is at the desk writing and working and looking at documents

Actress as Nurse E How are you?

Silence

The doctor wants to see you. (*She takes Mrs Manahan by the arm, very gently, and propels her to the Doctor*)

The Actress exits

Actor as Doctor E Do you know where you are?

Mrs Manahan No.

Actor Back in Germany.

Mrs Manahan Oh.

Actor The New York Authorities declared that, as you had been found in Berlin, you could be presumed to be German. The German Government agreed.

Mrs Manahan I see.

Actor You were sent here.

Mrs Manahan Oh . . .

Actor I want to ask you some questions.

Mrs Manahan About my life? That's quite easy. It is composed of endless questions.

Actor You say you are Russian?

Mrs Manahan Yes.
Actor Tell me about Russia.
Mrs Manahan What?
Actor Its history.
Mrs Manahan Modern Russia began, I suppose, with Ivan the Terrible. Then with Peter the Great came the great leap forward. He was determined to modernize Russia and ...
Actor What illnesses have you had?
Mrs Manahan As a child or since?
Actor Since when?
Mrs Manahan The Revolution.
Actor Since the Revolution then.
Mrs Manahan Tuberculosis of the left arm, pneumonia, and I am, of course, raving mad.
Actor Why do you say that?
Mrs Manahan I have delusions. You have patients who think they are Jesus Christ or the Pope or Napoleon. I think I'm the Tsar's youngest daughter, Anastasia ...
Actor From our observation here, there can be no question of insanity.
Mrs Manahan Oh but, doctor, I am violent—didn't the Americans tell you?
Actor A violent reaction to an assault on your liberty is not proof of insanity. I simply do not know what the American Authorities are talking about. You have a clear memory. You are well orientated. You have logical thought processes. You simply cannot be detained here against your will. So whenever you are ready, the nurse will make arrangements for you to leave.

Mrs Manahan gets up and slowly puts on the coat she wore when she first entered in Act I

The Actor stands at the back

The Actress comes in and sits to make notes

The Inspector—now the modern Inspector enters

Mrs Manahan And so again I was on my own. With the coming of the Nazis and the war I was at last forgotten. But after the war I was found again.
Inspector And more evidence was brought to light, much of it favourable. Whatever the Hesse family may say, the Grand Duke did in fact visit Russia in nineteen-sixteen. Army officers testified to seeing him in St Petersburg.
Mrs Manahan But Inspector, people can testify what they like. They can write books, plays, newspaper articles, but NOTHING, NOTHING will ever be conclusive.
Inspector I am a younger generation and I come to your case completely fresh. I have no views one way or the other. Anastasia's life can be proved up till her arrival in Ekaterinburg and your life proved from the time you were found in the canal, nothing can be proved between those two events.

Mrs Manahan That is the problem. It has always been the problem.
Inspector If we exclude your evidence, everything is just hearsay.
Mrs Manahan Everything.
Inspector Let us work backwards from the moment you tried to kill yourself. You jumped into the canal having run round Berlin.
Mrs Manahan Yes.
Inspector Lost.
Mrs Manahan That's right.
Inspector The name of the hotel you stayed in you had forgotten.
Mrs Manahan I never knew it.
Inspector You had crossed Europe from Bucharest with your brother-in-law.
Mrs Manahan That's right.
Inspector Who was never found again.
Mrs Manahan Never.
Inspector Nor were his mother and sister.
Mrs Manahan No.
Inspector Nor was the church you were married in in Bucharest.
Mrs Manahan No, it wasn't.
Inspector Nor any mention of your husband's death. Nor was the child registered.
Mrs Manahan That's right.
Inspector You will agree, therefore, that there is no evidence at all of your being in Romania.
Mrs Manahan None.
Inspector You arrived there after a journey lasting a year across Romania.
Mrs Manahan I can't prove that journey either.
Inspector So we can't prove that you were in Romania and we can't prove you crossed Russia. There remains the massacre. Now on this we have a mountain of evidence.
Actor as Soldier The whole of the Imperial family was assembled in the dining-room and were informed they were to be shot. The soldiers fired at them at once. Some were killed instantly, others ran round screaming. Then there was silence. One of the Grand Duchesses was still alive. She was stabbed thirty-two times.
Inspector Ah! So you were at the massacre?
Actor No, sir.
Inspector Who told you this, then?
Actor Court Inspector Tomashevsky.
Inspector And he was there?
Actor No, no. He was told by a person close to the Soviet Authorities.
Inspector Third hand. Quite inadmissible as evidence.
Actress as Secretary I was there, sir.
Inspector Who are you?
Actress I was a secretary at Ekaterinburg. At about four in the morning I was woken by Kleschev, the sentry, who was shouting in great excitement, "Tonight the Tsar's been shot!"

Inspector But that won't do. It's second-hand.

Actor as Prince Lvov Permit me. I was at Ekaterinburg at the time, and the massacre was terrible.

Inspector And you are?

Actor Prince Lvov. I can assure you the Bolsheviks spent the entire night inflicting blow after blow on them with bayonets before finishing them off. The room was literally a pool of blood.

Inspector But did you actually see the room yourself?

Actor Well, not exactly. It was common knowledge. I have seen the photographs, though.

Actress as Pathologist So have I. I am a pathologist and I have examined all the photographic evidence, and this photograph, for example, is evidence of a mild nosebleed, not of a massacre.

Actor I tell you they were bayoneted and shot.

Actress Not in this room, they weren't.

Actor A finger was found and photographed. It was identified as the Tsarina's.

Actress How? It would be decomposed.

Actor The bones were found and photographed as well. Look!

Actress There are not enough bones here for one body, let alone several. You see, we know a great deal more about mass murder in nineteen eighty than we did in nineteen-eighteen. The Reds had two days to destroy the evidence of the murder of sixteen people and this is scientifically impossible in the time.

Inspector But, madam, an eyewitness was quite explicit.

Actor When the bloody heap of bones was ready, we had built a fire. Arms, legs, heads and all were laid two layers deep. We drenched it all in petrol and acid and set it alight. Not a fingernail or a fragment of bone remained.

Actress That is quite impossible. Even in modern laboratory conditions such total destruction of human remains can't be done.

Actor as Prince Lvov If it couldn't be done, why did the Reds say they did it?

Inspector To terrify the local countryside into submission, of course.

Actor Certainly the Bolsheviks rejoiced in every horror story.

Inspector So did the Tsarists. They spread the same horror stories but for the opposite reason—to incite the local countryside to resistance. That's why the British Foreign Office Report, which claimed that only the Tsar and his son were killed, was suppressed. So, Mrs Manahan, the mistake my father's generation made was to accept the massacre as fact; simply because people said there had been a massacre they believed them and you know, I don't think . . .

Mrs Manahan (*interrupting firmly*) I am old, Inspector, and tired, Inspector. You can investigate this case to the end of time; it will make no difference. Either you believe me or you don't. I have ceased to care. I have at last made a new life. I have a husband, a legal name which no one can challenge. I repeat my first request to you, just leave me alone.

Inspector You told my father you never lied. So, Mrs Manahan, before you go, I am going to ask you one final question and you have only one thing to do. Just tell the truth as you say you always do. Was there a massacre at Ekaterinburg?

Mrs Manahan No.

Inspector No massacre?

Mrs Manahan Not at Ekaterinburg.

Inspector Not at . . .

Mrs Manahan Not at Ekaterinburg. I cannot tell you the rest.

Inspector But then no one will ever know the truth.

Mrs Manahan That's not quite right. I know the truth. And if I told you, you would not believe me. No, you would not believe me.

CURTAIN

FURNITURE AND PROPERTY LIST

ACT I

On stage: Couple of chairs
Table (to double as a desk). *On it:* a bell, telephone
Coat stand. *On it:* various hats, scarfs, coats

Off stage: Hospital bed

Personal: **Mrs Manahan:** coat, book, magazine, some mushrooms
Actor: file, 2 syringes, monocle, elegant walking-stick
Actress: books and magazines
Inspector: false moustache, newspaper

ACT II

On stage: As for Act I

Set: Reference book, hand-written notes on the desk

Personal: **Actor:** camera, spectacles, some legal papers, pen

LIGHTING PLOT

Property fittings required: none

ACT I

To open: Full general lighting

Cue 1 **Mrs Manahan:** "... what is it you want to know?" (Page 2)
Black-out, then Lights up on the **Actor** *and* **Actress**

Cue 2 **Mrs Manahan:** "... youngest daughter of Tsar Nicholas II of Russia." (Page 19)
Black-out except for a spot on **Mrs Manahan**

Cue 3 **Voices:** "How did you escape ...?" (Page 19)
Lights up on **Mrs Manahan** and the **Inspector**

ACT II

To open: Full general lighting

Cue 4 As the **Actor** and **Actress** exit (Page 38)
Lights down

Cue 5 **Mrs Manahan:** "Can I play with Alexis?" (Page 38)
Lights up on **Mrs Manahan**

EFFECTS PLOT

ACT I

Cue 1 **Actress:** "I recognized her. Just like that!" (Page 14)
Telephone rings

Act II

No cues

MADE AND PRINTED IN GREAT BRITAIN BY
LATIMER TREND & COMPANY LTD, PLYMOUTH
MADE IN ENGLAND